First Guide to Government

What's a Governor?

Nancy Harris

Heinemann Library
Chicago, IL

Photo research by Tracy Cummins and Heather Mauldin
Designed by Kimberly R. Miracle and Betsy Wernert
Printed in China by South China Printing Company

12 11
10 9 8 7 6

ISBN-10: 1-4034-9508-4 (hc)   1-4034-9514-9 (pb)

Library of Congress Cataloging-in-Publication Data
Harris, Nancy, 1956-
  What's a governor? / Nancy Harris.
     p. cm. -- (First guide to government)
  Includes bibliographical references and index.
  ISBN-13: 978-1-4034-9508-2 (hc)
  ISBN-13: 978-1-4034-9514-3 (pb)
 1. Governors--United States--Juvenile literature. 2. Governors--United States--Powers and duties--Juvenile literature. 3. State governments--United States--Juvenile literature. I. Title.
  JK2447.H37 2008
  352.23'2130973--dc22

                    2007010869

Acknowledgments
The author and publishers are grateful to the following for permission to reproduce copyright material: ©Alamy **pp. 5** (Jeff Greenberg), 16 (Glow Images); ©AP Photo **pp. 4** (Rob Carr), 6 (Steven Senne), 11 (Mary Ann Chastain), 12 (Chuck Burton), 13 (Mark Humphrey), 14 (Louie Balukoff), 15 (Don Ryan), 17 (Bob Child), 18 (LM Otero), 19 (Harry Cabluck), 20 (Ted S. Warren), 22 (Mark Humphrey), 23 (Ted S. Warren), 24 (The Sun/ Jacob Lopez), 25 (Rick Scibelli), 26 (Richmond Times-Dispatch/ P. Kevin Morley), 27(George Rizer), 29 (Evan Vucci); ©Redux **p. 28** (Globe Staff/John Tlumacki); ©REUTERS **pp. 7** (Hyungwon Kang), 9 (Jeff Zelevansky); Shutterstock **p. 8** (Chee-Onn Leong).

Cover photography reproduced with permission of Ken James/Corbis.

Every effort has been made to contact copyright holders of any material reproduced in this book. Any omissions will be rectified in subsequent printings if notice is given to the publisher.

Contents

Some words are shown in bold, **like this**. You can find out what they mean by looking in the glossary.

What Is a Governor?

The governor is the leader of a state government. The state government leads the whole state. The governor is **elected** (chosen) by people who live in his or her state.

★ The governor represents the state's people.

Each state has its own government. It is made up of people who are elected by **citizens** to lead the state. Citizens are people who live in the state and can vote for their leaders.

★ Citizens can vote for leaders in their state.

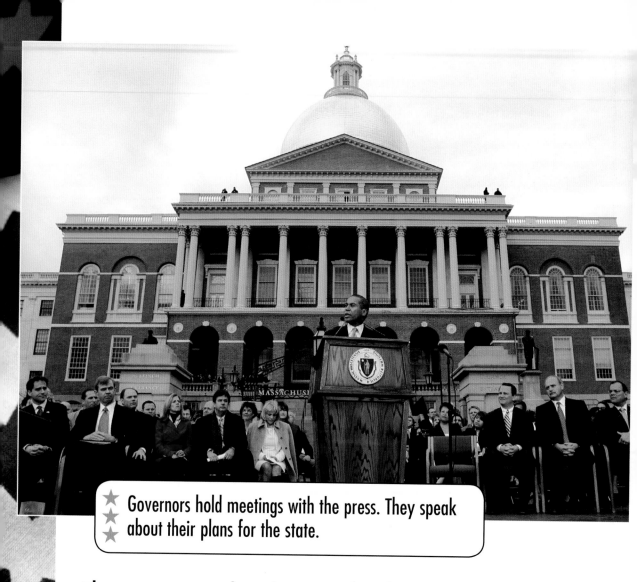

★★★ Governors hold meetings with the press. They speak about their plans for the state.

The governor makes decisions for the state. The governor also acts as a symbol for the state. He or she represents the beliefs of the state's people.

★ The governor meets with citizens to hear their concerns.

The governor speaks to **citizens** about matters of the state. For example, the governor might speak to the people in the state about plans to fight crime. The governor might speak about building new highways or improving business in the state.

The Governor and the State Executive Branch

The governor is the leader of the **state executive branch**. People in the state executive branch help the governor run the state.

★ The governor works in the state Capitol building.

The job of the state executive branch is to make sure the state **laws** are followed. Laws are rules people must obey.

governor

★★★ The governor meets with people in the executive branch. They discuss how to lead the state.

Executive Departments

The **state executive branch** has many **departments**. Departments are small groups of people with similar knowledge or interests. Each department has a certain job.

★ This chart shows a list of departments a state may have.

DEPARTMENT	JOB
Agriculture	Encourages and protects farming
Commerce	Gives permission for new businesses to open, responds to complaints from shoppers
Labor	Protects workers, helps people find jobs
Public Health	Gives health information and warnings to people
Transportation	Keeps roads and public transportation safe
Revenue	Collects taxes (money) from workers and companies in the state

★ Department members meet with others
★ to discuss important issues.

One department is made up of people who know about education. They make decisions about how to run the schools in the state.

In 2005, New Orleans, Louisiana was flooded after Hurricane Katrina. City workers helped clean up after the flood.

Some **departments** may help in an emergency, such as a flood. The governor and the departments work together to help with the emergency.

The state executive branch may have other groups that help run the city. For example, many states have an emergency management agency. This agency helps make plans for emergencies.

★★★★★ This is governor Phil Bredesen of Tennessee. He is meeting with the Tennessee Emergency Management Agency.

The governor chooses the people who lead the **departments** and groups. These people help the governor run the state.

★★★ The former governor of Washington state is congratulating a department leader on her work.

Working with the State Legislative Branch

The governor works with the **state legislative branch**. This branch makes **laws** (rules) for people in the state.

★★★ The state legislative branch is also called the state legislature.

Washington, D.C.

★ The federal government is in Washington, D.C.

State governments can make their own state **laws**. They must also follow the laws of the United States **federal government**. The federal government makes laws for the entire country.

The governor can give ideas for state laws. The governor can also ask for meetings with the **state legislative branch**. This may be done when the governor feels there is something that must be discussed right away.

Governor Rell of Connecticut is meeting with people in the state legislative branch.

Making State Laws

★★★ People in the state legislative branch meet to discuss a bill.

It takes many steps to make a state **law**. First an idea for a new law is brought to the **state legislative branch**. The idea for a law is called a **bill**.

People in the state legislative branch discuss the bill. Then they vote on it. If more people vote for the bill than against it, the bill is sent to the governor.

★ State legislators' votes may be shown on a board.

If the governor signs the **bill**, it becomes a state **law**. The governor can also veto (reject) the bill. The bill is then sent back to the **state legislative branch** to be looked at again.

★★★ This is Governor Gregoire of Washington state. She is signing a bill.

Planning the State Budget

The governor helps plan the state **budget**. The budget is a list of the money needed to run the state government. It also lists the money needed for state building projects and other costs.

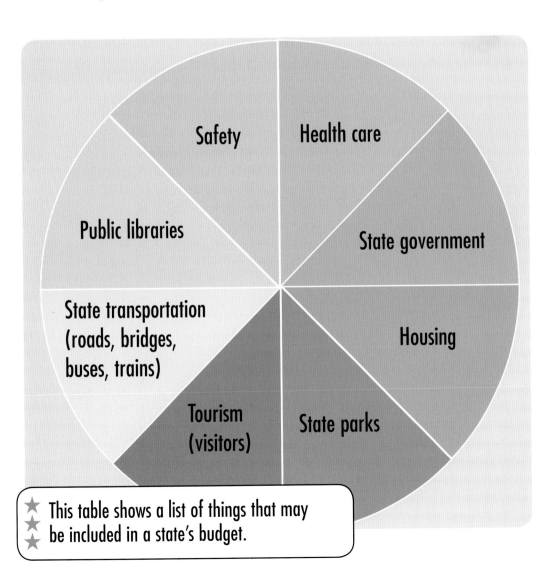

Safety

Health care

Public libraries

State government

State transportation (roads, bridges, buses, trains)

Housing

Tourism (visitors)

State parks

★★★ This table shows a list of things that may be included in a state's budget.

The **budget** is voted on by people in the **state legislative branch**. They must **approve** (agree with) the budget before it is used by the governor.

★ These legislators are placing their votes.

Working with the State Judicial Branch

★ Judges work in the state judicial branch.

The governor works with the **state judicial branch**. People who work in this branch decide if a **law** has been broken.

Judge

ANDREW W. GOULD
PRESIDING JUDGE

★★★ Courts are led by judges. They may decide if a law has been broken.

The **state judicial branch** is made up of courts. A court is a place people can go if they feel a **law** has been broken. The people who work in courts decide if the person is **guilty** of breaking a law. The punishment for breaking a law could be paying money or going to prison.

★★★ Governors may meet with prisoners to decide if they should give them a pardon.

The governor can **pardon** people for their crimes. If the governor gives someone a pardon, that person may no longer have to pay money or stay in prison.

Commander in Chief

The governor is the **commander in chief**. This means he or she is in charge of the state's National Guard. The National Guard is a group of military troops. They help protect the state.

★ Governors can meet with the state's National Guard.

★ The National Guard may help with security at airports.

The governor can call the National Guard when there is a state emergency. The governor can order them to protect an area in the state.

Running for Governor

★ Deval Patrick became governor of Massachusetts in 2007.

Each state has different **laws** that say who can run for governor. They also say how long the governor may serve. In most states, the governor is **elected** for a **term** of four years. In New Hampshire and Vermont, the governor serves a term of two years.

Leading Our States

★ Linda Lingle is the first female governor of Hawaii.

The governor is very important to the state. He or she is the leader of the state. The governor makes sure the state laws are followed. The governor represents the state's people.

Glossary

approve agree with

bill written idea for a new law

budget plan that shows how money will be spent in the state

citizen person who is born in the United States. People who have moved to the United States from another country can become citizens by taking a test.

commander in chief person in charge of the armed forces. This includes all the people who serve (work) in the state military.

department group of people who work together. People in each department have knowledge of a subject, such as education.

elect choose a leader by voting

federal government group of leaders who run the entire country. In a federal government, the country is made up of many states.

guilty responsible for a crime

law rule people must obey is a state or country

pardon officially release someone from punishment for committing a crime

state executive branch part of the state government that makes sure laws in the state are followed

state judicial branch part of the state government that makes sure laws in the state are understood

state legislative branch part of the state government that makes laws

term length of time a leader serves in a position

More Books to Read

De Capua, Sarah. *Being a Governor*. New York: Children's Press, 2004.

Firestone, Mary. *The State Governor*. Mankato, MN: Capstone Press, 2004.

Gorman, Jacqueline Laks. *Governor*. Milwaukee: Weekly Reader Early Learning Library, 2005.

Web Sites

Great Government for Kids has information about local government, state governments, and the federal government.
http://www.cccoe.net/govern/index.html

Visit PBS Kids' the Democracy Project to play fun games and learn all about how local, state, and federal governments run your city or town.
http://pbskids.org/democracy/mygovt/police.html

Index